Haunting Short Tales of Twila

J. E. Nicassio

FOR ALL YOU:
Witches, and ghouls, on Halloween.

SHORT, SHORT, STORIES each containing the key words

Twila, and key. The Haunting Short Tales of Twila was

originally published in the Trib Total Media 2008

The Purr-fect Deed

Twila Parker rushed out of her quaint suburban home in Sinner's Court, Nebraska, as she did every morning. She took in a deep breath, savoring the sweet smell of autumn.

The October breeze whispered in the air while the crisp colors of autumn rustled through her long blonde hair.

Twila lowered the mirror and puckered her lips to apply her lipstick and rudely ignored her neighbor's waves as she slid behind the wheel of her sleek, black BMW.

She backed out onto the road while checking her perfect face in the rearview mirror, not paying attention to a young mother pushing a stroller. She almost clipped her with the car.

Yep, that was Twila Parker for you: a forty-year-old, self-proclaimed real estate guru.

She was always looking for senior citizens unexpectedly in need of selling their homes. Once she got the poor souls in the palm of her freshly manicured hands, she conned them out of their property and their life savings, giving the property owner far less than the property was worth.

Twila could even convince them to use their Social Security checks to fix up the property before selling it to her. She had a way of talking the property owner into thinking it was a shrewd investment. Little did they know she was robbing them right under their noses! She made the

Grinch look like a saint.

As luck would have it, Twila just happened to find her way onto one of the most prestigious streets in the Hillcrest Pines neighborhood.

She came across a breathtaking mansion overlooking the city. It was a replica of an old medieval Tudor constructed of stone, Belgian block, and stucco.

The steep slate roof and stone chimney reminded Twila of the house Hansel and Gretel may have lived in. Of course, she had to have it!

Twila pulled her BMW up to the elegant, towering, cast-iron gate leading into the enormous piece of real estate.

She hit the button on the car door, and the tinted driver's side window slid down. Poking her beautiful blonde head out, her sapphire eyes noticed a

"For Sale by Owner" sign on the front lawn. Intrigued by the estate,

Twila slivered her golden-tan, size-eight body out of her BMW and stylishly strolled up to the sign. She slipped off her red Manolo Blahnik pumps for fear she might get them dirty. She began to read the sign.

FOR SALE BY
OWNER EBAY.
ESTATE SALE.

Twila turned her head right, then left, making sure no one saw, and yanked the sign out of the ground, sprinted back to her car, slipped her Manolos back on, and tossed the sign in the back seat.

She put her foot down hard on the gas and drove back to her office. She threw the office door open and went directly to her computer, walking right past her brother and business partner, Zed. without saying a word and logged on to the eBay auction site. After searching a few minutes, she found the advertisement.

For sale by owner. Bid starts $100 US dollars. Cotswold-style English Tudor, large piece prime property. Only stipulation -Previous owner left the home to her beloved stray cats. New owners will care for the cats the remainder of their lives. Includes contents of home.

While Twila was reading the description of the house, Zed, a tall, hefty man, leaned over she shoulder

Twila turned, seeing Zed's beer belly poking her in her face.

"Do you have to do that?"

"What are you looking at?" Zed followed Twila's gaze on the computer monitor.

"This Tudor being sold on eBay; the mansion on the top of old Harrison City-Export Road."

"Ooooh, the crazy old lady with all the stray cats who died last year." "What are you talking about?" Twila looked at her brother.

"It's the O'Reilly estate. Old Mrs. O'Reilly inherited millions from her grandparents. When her grandparents died twenty years ago, she moved in after her husband left her for a priest... yeah, a priest. The old bag never remarried and lived there by herself with all the stray cats in the neighborhood that no one wanted.

Rumor has it most are sickly and deformed. After the old lady died, not having any kids of her own, she left everything to her nieces and nephews, but for some reason they didn't want anything to do with it. They were afraid to put the cats down because some say the property is cursed, so they locked the cats up in the basement. The old lady was supposed to have lost her mind. Now, if I recall, in order to keep the mansion and all the money, the cats would have to stay."

"Hmmm... well, that's easy. Just put the cats to sleep?" Twila responded, hardly lifting an eyebrow.

"Nope. Look." Zed pointed to the computer screen. "See the fine print on the screen. It says "cats must have a yearly vet check."

"Well, there goes that idea."

Twila wrinkled her straight, narrow nose.

"I say we bid on it and cross that bridge when we come to it," Twila said, as she typed on her keyboard. "Let's start bid at $100.00."

Later that day the bid closed, with no out-bidders, making Twila and Zed the new proud owners of the Old Lady O' Reilly's Estate.

In the days that followed, Twila and Zed packed their bags and drove up the iron gates leading up to the O'Reilly Estate. Outside, standing before the Tudor, was the groundskeeper, Clyde Westin. His expression was grim and in his hand was an antique key ring.

"So you're the new owners of Mrs. O'Reilly's place." Clyde grimaced.

"Yes we are. Do you have the keys and contract?" she asked, holding out her hand.

"Here you are. You sure you want to live here? There are lots of crazy stories about this place."

"Stories? What kind of stories?"

"Strange things. Not sure. But I'd never want to live here."

"They're just that stories. I'm not going to listen to any rumors. This place is a master piece."

Twila smiled as she looked at the vision in front of her.

Zed carried Twila's bags into the mansion. She hollered and nagged at

Zed repeatedly about dragging her designer bags on the ground.

Did it ever occur to her that Zed might hate being her bag boy? Nevertheless, he did whatever Twila asked of him.

Over the year, Twila changed almost everything in the mansion. There was only one thing she kept the same; the lock on the room that caged Mrs. O' Reilly's cats.

Twila made sure she fed them every evening and gave them a clean bowl of water. They would meow and scratch at the door, but Twila followed the deed guidelines and never let them out. However, curiosity got the best of her one day.

It was Halloween, and Twila and Zed were celebrating their first year in the mansion. Twila decided to have a feast to celebrate their anniversary in their new home. She hired a chef to make all her favorites—a glazed ham and potatoes—- and had a designer come and decorate the mansion with all kinds of ghouls.

Twila always sparkled on Halloween, as most bitchy witches did. She changed into a black cat costume hoping trick or treaters would stop by.

On her way down to the basement, like she did every day to feed the cats dinner, as she did every day, she heard the cats meowing and scratching at the door.

For a brief moment, Twila pitied the poor cats that had spent the last year locked in that room. She pulled the lever on the door leading into the room where the cats were kept and out came the dinner tray from under the door. She emptied a can of Friskies in the bowl and glared at the gold lock that imprisoned the cats.

Twila thought to herself, what harm could be to let the cats out. She heard their meows get louder as if they were reading her mind. She took the antique key ring from her wrist and located the dark worn key that unlocked the door and held it in her hand. Then she took the key and put it in the lock and turned it. And the door flung opened.

Twila expected to see the mangy cats running out, grateful to be free, but she heard and saw nothing; not one cat appeared. Disappointed, Twila left the lock hanging from the door and turned and went back upstairs to finish preparing for her and Zed's Halloween feast.

Twila had everything ready. Pleased with herself, she sent the chef and the designer home.

The table was set with Mrs. O'Reilly's finest china, and the crystal wine glasses were full to the rim with expensive imported red wine.

The mansion was decorated with vampire bats, and spider webs were scattered on the walls. Zed played Halloween sound effects on the Bose sound system, and a few spiders dangled around the crystal chandelier. Twila even had a bright orange Jack 'o' lantern glowing in the front window for the trick or treaters to see.

Just when Twila and Zed were about to sit down to dinner, they heard the doorbell ring.

"Oh, hurry, it must be our first trick or treaters."

Twila beamed with delight.

"Come on; get the bowl of candy," Zed said with gleam in his eyes.

They both rushed to the door, but no one was there. Stunned that the trick or treaters decided not to come in, they proceeded to set the candy bowl down and returned to the dining room to enjoy their dinner.

When they were going into the dining room, they stopped in their tracks.

Twila stood in the entry way and scurried beside Zed, who was caught off-guard and was holding his chest.

Sitting at the dining room table were four figures. One was a ghastly sight with long, black hair. His skin hung over his body, mounds of flesh rolling off what seemed to be a man. He had huge, gold eyes that watched Twila and Zed curiously. He held on to the table and jumped with every move that Twila and Zed made.

HAUNTING SHORT TALES OF TWILA

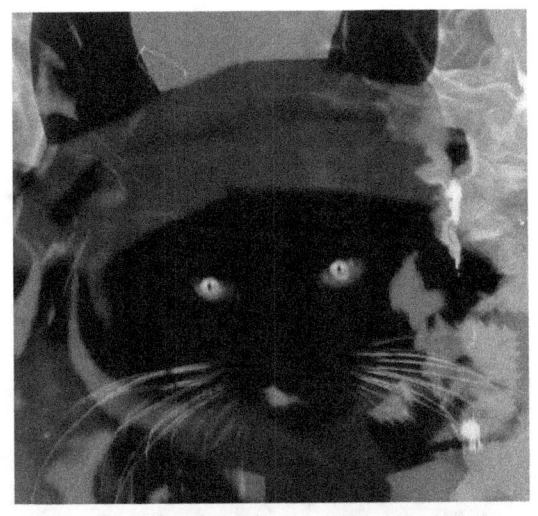

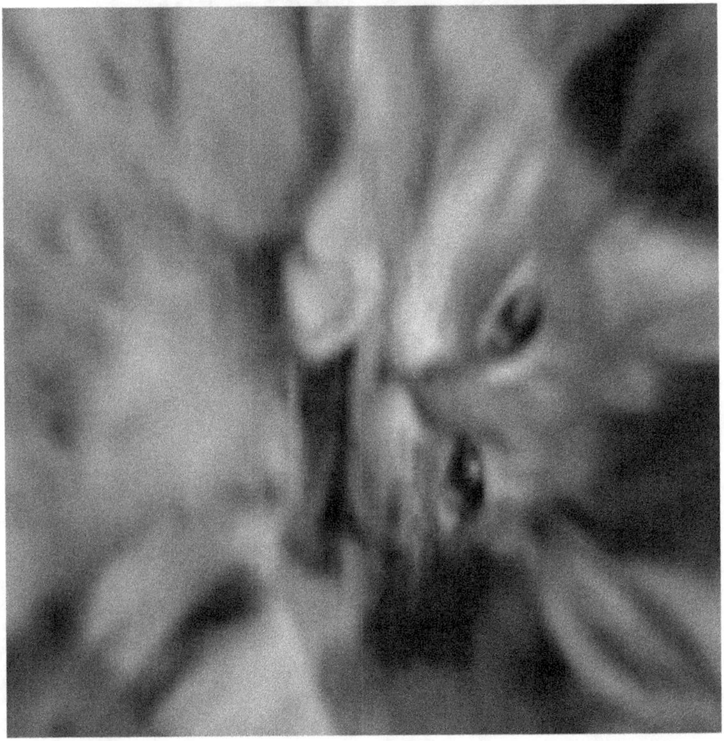

On the next chair was a man who had grey hair and huge, disgusting sores where hair had once grown.

His one eye hung by its socket. On the next chair, there was a long, lean man with dark, gray hair and large, snake-like yellow eyes; green snot coming from his nose. He smiled at Twila and lowered his head, showing an evil grin. To his right was a beautiful woman with long, blazing red hair and smoldering, blue eyes. She was holding a glass of wine.

The beautiful woman looked at Twila and smiled a graceful grin, showing her pearly white teeth with very sharp fangs.

"Love the kitty costume; so fitting," the blazing redhead said, raising her eyebrows.

Twila and Zed were too scared too move until the unwelcomed woman guest spoke again.

Her words came out of her mouth with a perfect low tone.

"Twila— my dear. Thank you so much for the fine wine and Halloween feast, but you should have not gone to so much trouble."

"Who're you and how'd you get in?" Twila screamed across the room

The black- haired man jumps and scurries out of the dining room on his hands and knees.

"Oh, Twila, I hate to be the one to break the news, doll, but did you read the fine print on the lease before you bought the mansion?"

"What fine print?"

Twila looked at Zed with anger. Zed shook his head in disbelief.

"On the lease, silly."

The red head got up and glided as

gracefully as any feline would do, and handed Twila a magnifying glass she took out of her pocket.

Twila hurriedly opened the drawer to the antique desk and pulled out the lease to the mansion.

It read:

Under no circumstance unlock the cellar door that encases the cats on Oct. 31st. The contract will be nulled and void.

Twila and Zed screamed! They held on to each other, kicking and screaming as the four grotesques creatures carried them down the eerie cellar steps and threw the two in the room and locked the door that had caged the sickly cats in darkness for so long.

Twila and Zed shrieked in terror and scratched at the door until their fingertips bled.

It was true; Old Mrs. O'Reilly had put a curse on the property. If anyone

unlocked door that held her beloved cat's captive on October 31st, it would release the cats onto humanity.
Her beloved cats would change form, and the ones who released them would take their place.

The four returned to the dining table and sat down. The redhead took a can of Friskies from her pocket and opened the can in silence. The whoosh of the air coming from the can when the medal lid flipped opened was all that was heard.

The blazing red-haired woman looked around at her hideous family with a mischievous smile gleaming upon her gorgeous face and said, "Pate,' anyone? Meow."

FOREVER IN TWILA

In the small multiplicity of Twila, there lives an average American family. A hard working man named Wilbur Mooney, works at a small insurance company, making ends meet. He sits at his desk, filing insurance claims. He has been doing the same job for the last 20 years. Each day, he leaves at exactly 5 p.m. and stops at the local pub for a beer, leaving at precisely 5:15 p.m.; he gets home at approximately 5:45 p.m.

Wilbur lives with his wife, Martha, and his son, Zed. Day after day, Wilbur comes home from work and finds his wife slaving over a hot stove; his son Zed is in the living room playing "MADDEN" on his Play Station 3.

On this particular day, Wilbur walks in the door and looks around at his home of 30 years, sees his wife of 31 years, and realizes how miserable he truly is.

Wilbur stands in the foyer, leaning against the front door. He loosens his tie and rubs his tired eyes, trying to make the image in front of him clearer, but all he notices is how his wife had let herself go. She looks like his mother instead of his wife. Wilbur walks in the living room and stares at his 21-year-old son, shaking his head.

"You should be working, you lousy bum," he said with a scowl.

His son only raised a hand and wrinkled his brow.

Wilbur went into the kitchen and held his nose, and then he took off his shirt and necktie and threw them over the kitchen table chair.

"What smells horrible?" he asked, looking at the food in the casserole dish.

"I made your favorite dish, roast beef and creamed potatoes, Wilbur," Martha said and went and kissed her husband on the cheek.

"Get away from me, woman. Your breath reeks of garlic," Wilbur yelled. He wiped his cheek with the palm of his hand and sat down at kitchen table.

"Where is my paper?" Martha put down the dish she had in her hand and went and fetched Wilbur's newspaper paper, like a dog.

"Get me a beer," Wilbur growled. "And my pills." Poor Martha jumped again.

"You forgot to get me my REMOTE! WHAT GOOD ARE YOU, WOMAN?" Wilbur said in a loud voice, making the cat at his feet hiss.

Wilbur, Zed, and Martha ate their dinner in silence. Martha cleaned the dishes with Zed's help, and Wilbur went into the living room, carrying his paper. He turned on the TV and fell fast asleep, as he did every evening after work.

The next day, when Wilbur woke, he was still sitting on the chair in the same white t-shirt he was wearing when he fell asleep. He looked around the house, calling his wife and son's name. They were nowhere to be found. He went in the kitchen to find everything spotless, but still he could not find his wife and son.

He went in his bedroom and then in the bathroom. Eventually, he turned on the shower. He showered as he did every day and got dressed for work. In the kitchen, he made himself some coffee, and he took a bagel from the fridge and some cream cheese, and ate his breakfast in silence.

Wilbur looked at his watch. "The darn thing stopped," he mumbled under his breath.

He grabbed his car keys and stomped out the door, started his Ford Geo and proceeded out the driveway.

Where was the postman that Wilbur honked at every day for blocking his way? It was strange. The children who usually waited for the bus and made faces at Wilbur were not at the bus stop. Where was the school bus that would stop with its flashing lights every day that made Wilbur late for work? He stopped and growled under his breath.

"Where are the little brats?"

Wilbur drove through the town of Twila until he got to the red brick building he worked at for the last 20 years. There were no cars in the parking spaces. Again, Wilbur mumbled to himself, "Where the hell is everyone?" Wilbur got out of his Ford Geo and walked to the entrance of the insurance company. No one was at the front lobby desk. The lights were off, and no one was there. He growled out loud again.

"Loretta," Wilbur yelled. The receptionist was not there. He turned and walked through the cubicles, and no one was at their desk. No phones were ringing or faxes faxing. Wilbur was shocked.

Was it a holiday, or did everyone call off work and didn't tell him? That must be it, Wilbur thought to himself. He was annoyed again and stomped out of the building, and got into his Ford Geo. His blood was boiling with rage.

When Wilbur got to his house, there was a "For Sale by Owner" sign on the front lawn.

"What's this?"

Wilbur pulls the sign out of the ground and sprints to the front door. He turns the knob, but it would not open. He juggles the knob, but it does not budge.

"Martha! Open this door immediately!" Wilbur yells behind the door.

"Zed, get your lazy ass down here!"

Wilbur grimaces and pounds on the door once more. Gradually, the door opens. Inch by inch, the door creaks wide open, but not a sound can be heard from behind the door.

The lights are dimmed.
Wilbur walks inside slowly. He wipes the beads of sweat that are forming on his brow.

"Martha," Wilbur said in a whisper. "Zed, what's going on?" The Laz-y Boy chair where Wilbur usually sit spin around, facing Wilbur.

In the chair sit an insanely beautiful woman with jet- black hair and golden skin. She is wearing a tiny skirt showing long, lean legs in black leather thigh-high boots.

"Hello, Wilbur," the woman says with a velvet, husky voice. She smiles, showing perfect white teeth.

"I've been waiting for you."

"Who the hell are you, and what are you doing in MY HOUSE?"

"Now, now Wilbur, calm down. You're not talking to Martha or Zed."

"Where are Martha and Zed? What did you do with them?"

"Martha and Zed aren't here, Wilbur. It's just you and me," she said with a throaty, sensual voice.

"Isn't that what you always wanted, Wilbur—a beautiful woman waiting for you at home?"

The dark haired woman stood up and walked slowly to where Wilbur was standing.

"Just you and me, Wilbur."

The beautiful woman licked her red lips then gave Wilbur an alluring smile.

"Get out of my house before I make you get out!"

"Wilbur, I would not do that if I were YOU!" The dark haired woman glowered. Wilbur, startled, backed up towards the door.

"Where are you going, Wilbur? Leaving so soon? I have something for you."

The dark haired woman unbuttoned her blouse and took her perfectly manicured hand and pulled out a shiny gold key from her cleavage.

"What's that?"

"It's a key to unlock that door."

She turned and pointed her long

finger in the direction of a big red door

that was not there before.

"Where did that door come from?'
Wilbur said confused.

"Oh, that's the door you've been waiting for, Wilbur.

The door to where all your fantasies are. Here, take it."

She held her hand out smiling.

"Uh- ok," Wilbur replied as he walked up to the dark- haired woman cautiously.

She brushed her voluptuous body up against his.

For a second, Wilbur flushed.

"There you go, Wilbur. Take it."

Wilbur took the key and clutched it tight, for fear he would drop it.

The gold key glistened, lighting up the palm of his hand.

"Unlock the door, Wilbur," she

whispered.

Wilbur walked up to the door and put the key in the gold lock. He turned the knob slowly. Just when he was about to open it, he stopped. Wilbur twisted to look at the dark- haired woman, but she had vanished.

"Where does the door lead?"

Wilbur looked around for the dark-haired woman, but there was no woman— just a hideous looking, tall amber creature with knife-like ears and blood red eyes. It reeked with a horrible smell of death.

"Wilbur, what do you think is behind the door? Do you think the key is to the gates of heaven, you stupid moron!"

Now standing right behind Wilbur, the creature was once again the black-haired woman, and she leaned over and pushed Wilbur.

He caught himself right before he

fell down a dark, winding passageway...

"Welcome to the doorway to hell. Let me introduce myself," the she-devil held out her hand. "I've been around for a long, long time just waiting for the likes of you. Pleased to meet you, Wilbur. You can call me Beelzebub, Satan, Lucifer, whichever you prefer.

We have an extended time to get to know each other better. How about forever! Last night, you accidentally took too many pills with that last beer you demanded from poor Martha. Wilbur, she gave it to you alright! Ha, ha haaaaa," the she- devil laughed. "If you thought your life was miserable before,

you have seen nothing yet!"
The beautiful she-devil pulled out a sharp dagger from her bosom, brought it to her lips and kissed it, and then kicked Wilbur straight in the rear.

Wilbur fell through the doorway as

the devil's laugh echoed throughout the little house. Wilbur held his ears and screamed as he descended to the sizzling depths of hell.

"Martha! ZED!" Wilbur squealed, just like a pig before it's roasted...

"You can scream all you want; they can't hear you, Wilbur!"

The devil leaned over the doorway, and with a slur, called down the hole,

"Honey, I'm home!" Then she followed after Wilbur through the doorway to hell.

SOUL WALKER

There must be a mistake, thought Twila Winters. Why would Aziria do this? Twila fought to keep from falling into despair. She was accused of witchcraft. Knowing the punishment, the realization that she would be burned at the stake overtook her and her despair turned to fury.

With only a trickle of moonlight as her guide, Twila hesitated, holding her breath. Her legs gave way and she stumbled. She picked herself up and started out again, as the terrifying sounds of hungry hounds not far behind pierced her ears. She cringed. Twila had travelled this path a hundred times, but at night, the hollow of the woods was a dark and sinister place. She turned, looking over her shoulder. The cold night air stung her lungs with each breath.

The seething chants of the mob echoed behind her as well, causing Twila to shudder. She rolled the silken fabric of her petticoat between her fingers, the same fingers that used to entwine within her lover's thick, black locks.

Twila could see the blaze of torches approaching. Her nostrils flared from the smell of burning ash. She watched as the swirling, fiery flecks flickered in the wind. The seared fragrance reminded her of what awaited her and she gasped, not sure which way to run.

"Aziria Savage, you will surely pay."

Her chest rose within her tight corset as she negotiated the dark path as fast as her feet could endure.

The night bestowed just enough waning moonlight to guide her; however, recent storms had blown debris across the wooded path, making each step to the sorcerer's lair perilous. The mob's ever-louder chanting heightened Twila's fears; panic overtook her, and she became disoriented.

Not paying attention to her footing, Twila stumbled on a dip in the ground, and fell into a clump of damp and thorny branches, tearing her bodice's lacy material and revealing her young skin.

With no strength left, she crawled on her hands and knees.

Dirt and blood covered her feet as she tried to stand. She hesitated, holding her hands to her ears, trying to stifle the mad chants of the mob. She managed to find her footing and ran toward the clearing, as t h e chanting of the townspeople grew louder. Out of the mist, the stone castle took shape.

Breathless, Twila staggered and threw herself against the door. As if it were expecting her, the door swung open to reveal the dimly lit entrance hall.

"Aziria! Come out, you...you coward!"

Twila trembled as her feet crossed the threshold, and her gaze immediately turned to the top of the stairs.

There stood a dark figure in black breeches and an open white shirt, revealing a smooth-skinned, muscular chest, unlike those of the other men in the Colonies who were fat and fleshy. It was the sorcerer himself, the roguish Aziria Savage.

"Really, Lia, what's all the fuss about at this hour?"

Leaning over the banister, Aziria grinned. His eyes lingered on her exposed ivory skin.

"Mmmm, are you in need of my services, my love? You couldn't wait; you started without me? Twila's hand went to cover herself.

"No, don't... I was just imagining how I would like to bite down on your shoulder ever so gently, but as memory serves me, you prefer a bit more force."

Twila gazed as if spellbound by his bewitching visage.

She pulls her eyes away momentarily, remembering why she was there.

"Stop...you had no right! How could you betray me like this?"

"Betray you? My dear, all I did was teach you the fine art of witchcraft. What you did with that power is not my doing."

Aziria gave Twila a crooked smile.

"...I did nothing; you were the one who used magic to silence the governor, not I."

Aziria lifted a muscular leg over the

banister and jumped onto the stairs below. "Now why would I do such a thing?"

"—they're going to burn me at the stake for something you did."

He made his way down the curved stairway and perched himself in front of Twila.

"My dear, what have they done to you?"

He removed the hand covering her exposed skin and lifted the torn bodice, brushing Twila's ripe flesh, taunting her.

"Don't touch me."

"Twila, you've gotten yourself in quite a bind."

"You are surely behind this."

Aziria lightly touched her soiled cheek with the back of his hand.

"What a shame, to waste such beauty."

She pulled away from his touch and closed her eyes for a moment then stepped forward until she was only inches from his face.

"Why? Why have you done this?" Her voice cracked.

"Revenge my dear; an eye for an eye, like the Good Book says. Your father owed me a life and yours only seemed fair."

"They think I'm a witch…"

"Are you not?"

"An apprentice—your student—yes, but…"

"Your father owed me."

"My father owed you nothing. Why do you insist he had your beloved killed?"

A single tear made its way down Twila's cheek.

"He did no such thing."

Aziria took Twila's chin in his hand and gently brought his lips to hers, letting his tongue find hers in a brief, but fervent kiss.

Twila pulled away.

"Aziria…Did I mean nothing to you?"

She remembered how he held her in his arms, the way he pleased her for hours before satisfying his own needs.

He nodded with an evil smile; she felt his wickedness.

Was she wrong about him? Was he as evil as the Puritans and her father suspected? She couldn't believe it was all for revenge.

"No—I don't believe you!" she cried. Aziria's smile turned colder still.

"Your father killed my wife, whom I adored, and my unborn child, my heir, whom I will never hold; a child who will not carry on my legacy. They will be avenged, my dear, though I will miss the taste of your lips—like sweet nectar, so delicate—and, of course, that beautiful body of yours."

The townspeople were pounding at the door, but Aziria did nothing except watch Twila's shattered look.

The door broke open, filling the threshold with a crowd of rowdy men and women; some carrying torches, others sticks.

The leader was a minister, Twila's own father, holding a Bible tight in his grip.

"W-would you be so kind as to release this witch, Mr. Savage?" His words were slurred with fear.

"Father…no, I beg you." Twila began to tremble.

"Yes, release the witch!" the crowd roared. Their fury was almost as evil as their idea of what Aziria was.

"Please father—I did nothing," she said, her eyes pleading with him, but the minister refused to meet her gaze.

In that moment Twila knew that her

father, though he feared Aziria's powerful magic, would not hesitate to make an example of her—his own daughter—for following the desires of her flesh.

"Release the witch."

"By all means…take her," Aziria said, turning his back to the crowd.

Twila called out one last time, "Aziria, what kind of monster are you?"

Aziria turned around and said in a low whisper, "The worst kind…righteous and not pure of heart by any means."

* * * * *

Aziria stood silently as the crowd tore Twila away, contemplating his last words to her, and his revenge. He could not think of anyone else who would have wanted him and his wife dead except the Puritan minister, or the governor. Magic had long been thought the work of the devil; Salem was holding witch trials every other day.

He had not lied; he would miss Twila's lips. In their time together, Aziria had become quite fond of her innocence; it pleased him more than he'd expected. She had been an excellent pupil, quick to learn—not only in the black arts, but also in the bedroom.

He thought back to when his ship had arrived in the colonies; the governor and the Puritans had bristled at his arrival. They knew right away he was not like the other pilgrims, simply hoping for a new life in America.

He had a reputation for being skilled both in the black arts and with ladies of wealth and royalty.

Aziria didn't arrive in the Colonies alone; he came with his two servants and his wife, Sarah. Instead of coin,

Aziria paid talented mason workers' passage to America in return for their talents. A castle fit for a king was built of stone and the finishing touches were added with a little of Aziria's wizardly contributions.

Aziria, born of privilege and a descendant of Merlin, was known all across Europe. His services were obtained by the King's court on more than one occasion. His only motivation to leave the old world was his wife Sarah. As hard as Aziria tried, his magic couldn't sow his seed. His wife's womb was barren. When a midwife learned the natives of America knew of herbs and potions to aid in fertility, she sent word to Aziria.

The sorcerer and his wife set out on the next ship to America in hopes of trading gold for herbs, and that the herbs would eventually fill his wife's belly with a child.

When Aziria stepped off the ship, he could see Twila there gazing at him. After Aziria's beloved died suddenly, Twila became his main objective.

His grief soon turned to seduction, and Twila's innocent, girlish spying while he bathed at Willow's Beach became his only entertainment. Of course, he knew she would be there, so he purposely stood at attention without a stitch of clothing for her virgin eyes to see.

Knowing the young lady was watching only made Aziria more eager to have her. Twila, submissive to his every command, obeyed Aziria without caution. Some things Aziria's wife would have never done, Twila was eager to do. She offered her body and her soul without hesitation.

Aziria enjoyed Twila more than he'd enjoyed any other woman before. He would miss the fire between them and their passion they shared. He had soon begun to look forward to their time together—time he would miss when she was dead.

But he would never admit to loving Twila.

* * * * *

Midnight was approaching as Professor Melinda Cartwright sped to Salem's Paranormal Society; she was late for the weekly meeting at the university. Minutes ago, Melinda had received a mysterious call from a man claiming to be Aziria Savage; a man Melinda knew in a previous life.

Melinda began investigating the paranormal after she died in a car accident and was brought back to life minutes later. When she was resuscitated, Melinda remembered another life she had led in which her name was Twila Winters. She not only remembered dying; she remembered burning at the stake. And she remembered the man who had put her there: Aziria Savage.

After the accident, fleeting memories of her past life haunted her every day. Twila's life took over Melinda's mind and memories.

Some of the strongest memories were of Twila's first sight of Aziria, and of the moment they first met. Vividly, Melinda recalled Aziria's captivating physique. Not only did his alluring charm arouse her, a naïve eighteen-year-old girl, he mystified her with his unusual looks.

Most men of the time wore a moustache and beard, but Aziria was smoothly shaved, revealing a chiseled face that was almost too pretty for a man. Most men of the colonies wore doublets to the chin, but Aziria Savage wore bright linen shirts, open to the waist, further Enraging the Puritans. He would grin as he caught someone's eye, clearly enjoying taunting the men and teasing the women, who would blush traipsing by him.

Twila remembered hiding in the trees at Willow's Beach, ashamed of herself yet unable to tear her gaze from the charismatic stranger's naked body. At first, she didn't understand what she was feeling and ran home to meditate on a Bible verse, believing the Devil was its cause.

Each day, her desire for Aziria increased until Twila thought she couldn't take the longer any longer.

Then, one day while out picking berries, Twila lost her way during a sudden windstorm—a windstorm Aziria had brewed himself.

Under his spell, she ended up footsteps away from his castle, where the wizard himself stood in his garden, his back to her. She watched with curious eyes as Aziria bent toward the earth. Incantations of magic poured out of his lips, and as he spoke the words, a single weed turned into a beautiful white rose bush.

"Well, well, what do we have here?" Aziria asked, turning and approaching Twila with a seductive grin.

"Sir…The storm, I mean no intrusion. I was picking berries and the path leading to my father's farm has blown over with branches."

"Is that a fact?" He took a strand of hair that had fallen from her bonnet onto her cheek between his fingers. "You admire my roses?"

"They are beautiful, Sir."

"Not as beautiful as your ruby lips."

Twila blushed, unsure how to respond.

"How did you change the weeds into roses? Is it witchcraft?"

Aziria Savage laughed.

"I'm no witch, my dear. Witches are women. I'm a wizard. Why don't you come with me and I'll show you?"

He smiled, holding out his hand within it a shiny gold key.

Twila blushed and shyly took her hand in his, completely at his mercy.

It was then she knew Aziria Savage would change her life forever—the moment she walked over the threshold into his dark seductive world of magic.

* * * * *

Present

After the car accident, Melinda went
to several therapists hoping to find the
answers to these memories.

Not until she found one who
practiced past life regression therapy
did she truly believe she was, in fact,
the reincarnation of Twila Winters.

Through hypnosis, Melinda told
the therapist in detail the memory of
her horrible death by fire.

She learned the man she kept
seeing in her memories was Aziria
Savage, the man who had turned her
over to those who burned her at the
stake.

Melinda didn't know why her
earlier life now haunted her beyond
reason. All she understood was—she

was cursed.

The phone calls, on the other hand, had started many years back, before the accident. It wasn't until now that she put the two together.

She checked her rearview mirror; headlights—someone was tailgating her. Putting her foot to the accelerator, Melinda made a rapid right turn down the alley beside the university.

Having lost the vehicle after a few more quick turns, she pulled into the university parking lot.

Puzzled, she thought again of the phone calls. Could the phone calls and the person tailgating her be related, she wondered?

The meeting had already ended; members brushed by Melinda as they left Jacob Night's office. Jacob Night, her trusted colleague and friend, knew of Melinda's past life. With a raised brow, he watched Melinda rush in.

Salem's Paranormal Society was a small group of professors and students who believed in the existence of paranormal activity.

The Society was a non-profit group that investigated unnatural occurrences.

What was happening to Melinda was exactly the kind of phenomenon the group would investigate, but this was too close for comfort. It was a good thing the meeting had ended, for Melinda wasted no time in stopping Jacob.

"Good to see you could make it tonight," Jacob said mockingly.

"Jacob—it's starting."

"What is?" he asked, gathering his paperwork. Melinda and Jacob had tried to date, but although she cared for Jacob, she could never completely give herself to him.

Every time she started to get close to him, memories of Aziria Savage would come rushing in, taking over her thoughts and her body, making it difficult for her to love him, or any man for that matter. Any hope of a real relationship was gone.

"I got a phone call from Aziria Savage."

"How do you know it's Aziria? Could it be a trick?"

"I just do. It's his magic. I can feel it penetrating me. I know it's him, and this time he will be the one damned."

Melinda brushed by Jacob, but he stopped her with a tug of her arm.

"Melinda, what are you planning to do? If he's as dangerous and powerful as you claim, how will you destroy him?"

Jacob's dark eyes peered deep into Melinda's crystal blue ones.

"Especially if he's somehow managed

to stay alive." He loosened his grip.

"How will I destroy him? With the same vengeance as when he let me burn at the stake—or should I say, let Twila burn at the stake. And maybe, just maybe, this curse to relive that horrible death will end," she said bitterly.

"You believe he's the cause? Then you'd better take this," Jacob went to the filing cabinet and took out an ancient box.

He unlocked it with a key from his pocket. "I've been keeping this for just this occasion."

"You have?"

"Why don't you let me go with you?" he asked as he unlocked the box. He took out a small cloth; within it was a golden dagger.

"No...I have to do this myself."

"This will kill any wizard."

He handed Melinda the dagger.

Melinda looked at the weapon in awe.

"You have a golden dagger and sheath?"

"Of course—you never know when you may have to slay a sorcerer," Jacob joked.

"Where did you get this?" Melinda let her fingers glide across the sharp shiny blade.

"It was supposedly taken from the tomb of Merlin's arch-nemesis, Morgan le Fay."

"Then it's the enemy of Merlin's descendants as well."

"King Arthur's hire took it as a souvenir. Legend says Celtic gods have blessed it."

"Well then…if the gods have blessed it, I shall take it." Melinda took the dagger and sheathed it, placing it securely in her boot.

"Be careful with that."

"I'm not an enemy of Morgan le Fay." Melinda gave Jacob a smile as she lowered her pant leg.

Melinda knew Savage would show himself tonight; she could feel his presence deep within her soul.

She decided to go to the very spot where her former body was burned. It was not far from the university, at an old graveyard right outside of Salem.

It was just before three in morning— the witching hour, when lost souls wander the night—when Melinda pulled her car to the side of the road. She turned off the ignition and slowly stepped out.

It was dark, and with only the stars to light her way, Melinda strode toward an old wooden fence leading into the abandoned Salem graveyard.

Melinda knew exactly where her grave lay. Hers was among a group of other lost souls. She had come to this spot many times before and every time she found it amusing.

The graves were marked with an upside-down cross, signifying the rejection of Christ; a sign put there by the Puritans as a reminder for future generations that witches were buried there.

As always, when Melinda saw the cross, she began to laugh. "Puritans—Damn them to hell."

Fear stood in anyone's way if they had any inclination to turn the cross right side up. Even in this century, Salem's superstitious, God-fearing people believed they would be struck down by God for doing such a thing. Melinda laughed again.

"That amuses you. What you really wanted to say was 'Fuck them all to hell," a male voice said.

Melinda turned, looking in the direction

of the voice. "Who's there? I have a weapon."

"Of course you do…the golden dagger from Morgan le Fay's tomb, right, Twila?" The voice was louder, more distinct. "I have waited hundreds of years to feel your soul again."

"Show yourself!" Melinda shouted into the dark.

A man came into view, but it wasn't who Melinda expected to see.

He was taller and more defined than she remembered, his body bigger and more muscular, and his face more beautiful than Aziria Savage—the man who had loved her. The man she saw was definitely not Aziria; she backed away.

"It is I, Twila—Aziria—I mean you no harm," the man said.

His voice was different than she remembered, but it had the same authority and sensual rhythm as Aziria's.

Melinda strode slowly toward the speaker until his face was inches away. She remembered when he kissed her for the last time and how she had loved it, even as she hated him for it.

"Aziria?"

"Yes. And here you stand before me, but you go by the name Melinda Cartwright and your raven hair is now spun copper; your lips ruby red, and so plump.

And your breasts...fuller, and your hips wider, more sensual, not the narrow hips my Twila had—not that I mind."

They stood close, not touching, their breaths heavy.

"You betrayed me, Aziria. Why?" Melinda choked back tears.

"I was tricked. It wasn't your father who killed my beloved; it was the wizard Dorcas. I know that now. He feared my power was exceeding his own and he wanted me dead; the slaves he hired put the poison in my wife's chalice instead.

I thought your father did it because of the witch trials. I knew he thought I was the ringleader."

"So you used me to avenge your wife by having my own father slay me, and it was all for nothing. How did you learn this to be true?"

"When the mob took you to the stake, I realized you meant more to me than my thirst for revenge. I went after you to save you, but when I got there— it was too late. All the magic I possessed couldn't save you, but I wasn't the only one who had come to your side."

He paused, rage twisting the features of his unfamiliar new face.

"Dorcas came to gloat. He was the one who killed my wife, but the poison had been intended for me. He told me in detail how he came to my lair and stood before you and me as we slept in my chambers, entwined in each other's arms after making love. He was going to take my eyes from their sockets and claim my magic as his own. However, you woke and his plan was ruined. Twice he failed. Now, I will pay him a visit and avenge both my wife and you!"

"You came for me." Melinda wrapped her arms around her chest.

"Yes…I did. I've been trying to find you for hundreds of years. Before I was cursed, Dorcas captured me and killed me over and over. I used every ounce of magic to 'walk in' to another's body, to reincarnate to find you."

"You had me burned at the stake," Melinda hissed. She kicked Aziria's shin and sprinted toward her car. Aziria fell backward, stunned. He recovered and stood bent over, holding his leg.

"Do you know how painful that

was?" Tears welled in Melinda's eyes.

With a raised hand, Aziria moaned an incantation into the night air.

He walked slowly toward Melinda, who was now paralyzed by the spell he had cast.

She tried to move, but her free will was compromised by his magic. Beads of sweat began to form on her brow as she struggled to reclaim control.

Aziria strode to her and pushed her onto the trunk of her car. He took her hands and entwined them within his. She felt his magic release her, but she was still under his magnetic spell. This time, however, witchcraft had nothing to do with it.

"Twila, don't you remember how I taught you the fine art of love-making? I remember how you used to call my name…"

"As I recall, it was sex you taught

me; love had nothing to do with it."

He brushed the skin behind her ear with his warm breath. "How you pleaded with me for release; do you remember? Tell me, Twila; you do remember; I know you do."

Aziria let his hand glide over her chest.

"I pleaded with you to let me go."

"Tell me how you used to moan in bliss. I remember how you wanted me."

"I moaned…because I was scared." Her breath was heavy.

He slowly unzipped her jeans, letting his hand stay there just under the fabric. A light sound escaped her lips.

"Ah, you do remember me."

He took his hand from her jeans realizing what he did, Melinda clamped her thighs together and struggled beneath Aziria's hands.

"I remember the monster who ate my

heart, and let me burn at the stake," Melinda said in a whisper.

"What I ate was not your heart, my dear," he groaned with a hint of a smile.

"You're a pig who took advantage of a naïve girl's innocence."

"You were a willing participant."

"You bewitched me!"

"On the contrary, I did no such thing…no magic…ever. Not to you. You wanted me, just as much as you want me now."

"Never again."

"I went to save you, but it was too late…You were already gone. Your father couldn't live with what he had done and hanged himself that very night. Before your father died, I vowed to him I would avenge your soul, but he cursed me to never rest in peace; as punishment, my soul would not rest until I found you."

"My father was a man of the cloth; he would never have cursed you."

"Was he truly?"

"I thought you said you used your magic to reincarnate."

"Not exactly…give me a break; it's been a few hundred years." Aziria groaned. "I stepped into the body of a soul on Earth who was going to take his own life— upon his death, my damned soul would walk in his body.

His soul would move on to rest in peace, but I would claim the body and live out the remainder of his pathetic life. I did this again and again. Each life I took on, I vowed to find you, each life leading me closer to you.

I watched you burn to death…but before you died, I used all my power to place a spell upon your soul so you would never truly die, but be reincarnated until we found each other once again. Each time I would get close, you would die, only to be reborn," Aziria whispered near her ear.

"And I longed to kill you for years," Melinda moaned back.

Aziria released her and raised his hand to her bosom. He gently unbuttoned her blouse.

"Twila, you may be in another woman's body, but your soul still belongs with mine. I know you as I've always known you."

His touch made her body shiver; she remembered how she enjoyed his pleasure and, surrendering to his magic, she gave in to his advances.

She took his thick locks in her hands, pulling him closer. Her legs began to go weak. He might be in a different body, but his touch was that of the Aziria she longed for.

Hearing his name, Aziria found his way to her rosy lips and forcefully kissed her, beckoning her to succumb to his power.

She didn't fight his kiss, but welcomed it.

Then, like a bolt of electricity, Twila felt the heat of the flames that had melted her flesh to the stake, and she pushed Aziria off her. Dizzy, she fell to the ground, unable to grasp what was transpiring around her as darkness took her.

Aziria took hold of her, trying to bring her back to her senses. He knew what was happening—Dorcas was the cause.

He could feel Dorcas' magic pulling at him and he knew he had only a few hours to find the wizard and destroy his evil before he would have to walk again.

Melinda stirred long enough to tell Aziria to take her to Jacob's office at the university—Jacob had told her earlier he would be there working late on a research project. They needed to find a way to lure

Dorcas out of hiding. Jacob was all too willing to help Melinda who was coming in and out of consciousness, but Aziria mistrusted Melinda's colleague. He was *too* helpful.

"Take this, Melinda." Jacob held a glass of orange-colored liquid to Melinda's lips.

"What are you giving her?" Aziria asked, taking the glass from Jacob.

He brought it to his nose; it was odorless. It was then Aziria had a vision of Jacob showing Melinda the dagger.

The vision showed him what Melinda hadn't seen: after she left his office, Jacob turned into the evil wizard he truly was.

He was hoping when Melinda used the dagger, all of Aziria's magic would come into his evil possession for eternity, leaving Aziria powerless.

Aziria quickly sent the poison flying through the air. The glass shattered on the floor. Melinda lay on the office couch; the leg of her jeans raised just enough   to reveal the golden   dagger. Aziria wasn't the only one who saw it.

"Killing her when you're so close to finding your apprentice after all these decades," Dorcas said. "What a pity. A better way to make you suffer."

"Does my magic mean that much to you, Dorcas?"

Dorcas leapt for the dagger and snatched it from Melinda's leg. Aziria reached for Dorcas, trying to subdue him, but he slipped in the spilled poison and the dagger went flying to the floor, out of his reach.

"Why, Dorcas, why?"

"Why wouldn't I want your

power? You were becoming too powerful."

"So you destroyed three souls in order to possess it!"

"Let's not forget about your unborn child."

With that, Aziria lifted his hand and threw a ball of fire in Dorcas' direction. Dorcas ducked and the fireball knocked over a glass case holding antique leather-bound books, shattering the glass.

The fireball disintegrated behind Dorcas on impact. Dorcas threw a few fireballs of his own, lighting the room in red and blue glittering light.

Melinda awakened briefly to see the two men fighting.

"Aziria! You tricked me!" Melinda said in a strangled sob.

Believing Aziria was being deceptive, she went for the dagger.

Melinda crawled across the floor, grabbed the dagger, and managed to stand. As soon as the dagger was in her palm, she staggered, shocked.

"Twila no!" Aziria gazed at her with anguish.

"What's happening?" Melinda whispered to herself.

Spellbound, she stared at the dagger. Spheres of various colors radiated within her palm.

The dagger in her hand had magic of its own—magic that broke the spell.

Twila could see Jacob as he truly was, and in her vision Jacob's body began to transform.

His limbs pulsated and spun, revealing the horrid wizard who, she now knew, had caused all of her grief.

With the dagger still in her clutches, she lunged toward Dorcas. Caught off guard, Dorcas couldn't avoid her deadly thrust.

Like a wildcat, Melinda used the dagger to rip open Dorcas' throat. Aziria had raised his hand to throw another fireball when the room began to glow.

It was as if a poison was released through Melinda's veins; she collapsed onto the floor.

Aziria's body began to tremble. He felt himself transform into his own familiar flesh.

He peered down at his hands as they shook. He strode quickly to a piece of the broken glass that lay on the floor. Looking back at him was the Aziria he remembered.

His black hair hung in waves around his face, and his blue eyes sparkled. Relived he was the youthful Aziria and not his true age, he sprinted to the couch and picked up Melinda, who was now his beloved Twila, her beautiful spun copper hair now an exotic midnight black.

With the magic of two wizards, Aziria was more powerful than ever, and he knew exactly where Twila now lived.

He picked her up in his arms, carried her to her car, and drove to her apartment.

* * * * *

Twila awakened to the sight of her former mentor and lover. She let her eyes focus on the image of Aziria sitting in the loveseat across from her. The shirt he was wearing was unbuttoned, showing the smooth, rippled chest she remembered.

She rubbed her eyes…. Was she seeing right? This wasn't the man she had seen earlier, the man she presumed was the soul-walker of the wizard who stole her life.

She watched him sleep, each breath

he took sending a chill through her. She slowly lifted the cover and noticed her clothes had been removed.

How dare he take them off her while she slept? She took the sheet from her bed and wrapped it around her naked body.

The room was darkened and the only light came from the streetlight across the way.

Melinda tiptoed to her dresser drawer and took out the small pistol she kept in case of intruders.

She turned to look at Aziria, making sure he was still asleep. She crept toward him and stood over his sleeping body as she thought for a moment.

How she had longed for this day. She knew now he must have been lying to her at the graveyard; he had used his magic to trick her again before changing back into his familiar self. So many lifetimes she had waited for this moment.

She pulled the hammer back with her thumb and placed the barrel right under Aziria's handsome, chiseled chin.

She watched his pulse throb and, for just an instant, she paused.

Aziria, too quick, stole the gun from Twila and threw it across the room. He pulled her onto his lap.

The sheet fell to her waist. Startled, Twila pulled it back. Ignoring her modesty, Aziria pulled her tightly to him, wrapping his strong arms around her, causing Twila to draw in a long breath and fall into his chest.

She felt her heart pull. It was truly her Aziria, her teacher, her lover, whom she had loved and hated for so many years.

"What magic did you use to trick me again, you demon?" Twila choked back tears.

"Twila, I did not trick you," His breath was close to her ear.

"The spell is broken; see for yourself. Dorcas had you under his power, but he has you no more."

He pushed Twila off his lap and stood.

"It wasn't a dream?" Twila straightened, dropping the sheet that covered smooth youthful skin. Her raven hair revealed just enough to make Aziria smile a devious grin.

"It was no dream; Dorcas is dead. You slit his throat with King Arthur's dagger. The same one you wanted to use on me, my love."

Aziria pushed aside a strand of hair covering one of Twila's cheek. Twila's chin leaned in toward his hand.

"Is it true? Dorcas is no more," Twila repeated wonderingly.

Her face was flushed and the old

familiar ache was beginning to burn in the hallow of her stomach. She wanted him.

He clearly knew it. Her hand found his belt and slowly unbuckled it.

Aziria tried to contain his pleasure. He took her hand away and tenderly kissed each of her fingers, and then he let his lips and tongue find the delicate spot behind her earlobe.

She moaned when he kissed her shoulder, pausing to look in her eyes.

"Twila, how I've missed you."

He continued kissing her, gliding his warm tongue along her shoulder blade, making his way to the curve of her bosom.

She pulled away from his touch, wrapping the sheet tightly around her again. She looked down at her long raven hair and immediately strode to the mirror over her dresser.

"It's as if I never died. I am the same. I don't understand how this is possible."

Aziria stood behind Twila, looking

at her in the mirror.

Their eyes locked.

"The instant you killed Dorcas, the curse was broken. My wife was avenged, and your father's spirit may have forgiven me for seducing his daughter.... Dorcas was the true cause of our anguish."

"My father was a coward."

Aziria smiled.

"It doesn't matter now. We have a second chance; we can make magic together forever."

Aziria took the sheet from Twila and let it fall to the ground. "I don't want you to be my pupil, but my equal."

Aziria leaned in and kissed Twila's neck.

"Aziria, finish teaching me what I need to know."

Aziria laughed his roguish laugh.

"You don't need to be taught, my

love…You know what exactly to do. But if you insist."

"I insist, although I may have a few new magic tricks of my own to teach you."

"Only if you promise not to burn a hair on your beautiful head," he moaned in her ear.

"The only thing burning is the fire I have for you." With that, he took her in his arms.

He laid her down on the bed. His smooth, rippled chest glowed in the darkness. His magic lit up the room. Twila smiled, watching him.

Her body craved his; she wanted him more than she had wanted anyone in all of her lives.

He stood there, strong and masculine. She looked up to see Aziria smiling. She had never seen anything so wonderful since the last time they had been together, so many lives ago.

"Twila, I've missed you so," he whispered, right before he pulled her into his arms.

"Aziria S-savage, don't every betray me again…." Aziria looked at her once more before he leaned in and put his lips on hers.

"Ever again," Twila said between breaths.

"I've been counting the years without you and you're not going to talk now."

He hovered over her naked body and bent over, pressing his lips to hers.

They woke entwined in each other's arms.

"Twila…"

He breathed a few words of magic. A white rose appeared between his fingers.

"For you, my love."

"You never cease to amaze me, my lord."

"No—you're my equal now; I meant it."

He grazed her collar bone with his lips.

One thing a wizard cannot do, Twila recalled suddenly, is use his magic to create love. This love between them, then, was real.

With that realization, Twila relaxed, convinced at last that Aziria meant what he said.

"Hmm, I forgot…Well then, I demand you eat your breakfast and don't be shy about it," Twila said with a seductive smile.

"With pleasure," he growled, lifting the covers over his head to enjoy his breakfast, devouring every morsel.

Author Bio

J. E. Nicassio was born and raised in Pittsburgh, PA. She is a strong believer in reincarnation and anything paranormal.

www.authorjenincassio.com, or connect with her on Facebook.
ttps://www.facebook.com/jenicassio?ref=hl

Other great books include: From The Sky Rocky the Rockefeller Christmas Tree and Louis Joseph's Ooh Rah.

https://www.amazon.com/Rocky-Rockefeller-Christmas-Jennie-Nicassio/dp/0692771875/ref=sr_1_1?ie=UTF8&qid=1472788485&sr=8-1&keywords=rocky+the+rockefeller+christmas+tree

Soul Walker the original Cursed to Live Again published by Cobble Stone press
https://www.amazon.com/Cursed-Live-Again-Ava-Malino-ebook/dp/B00AQKDY48/ref=sr_1_1?ie=UTF8&qid=1473030983&sr=8-1&keywords=cursed+to+live+again

Coming Soon: The sequel to From The Sky-Equinox and Aurora's Curtain.